The Night the Ducks Got Loose

Charles Mountford

Pendas

The Night the Ducks Got Loose

Pendas Poets Series # 16
Series Editor Penn Kemp

hmtb ISBN 0-920820-73-5
CD ISBN 0-920820-74-3
book+CD set ISBN 0-920820-97-2

Pendas Productions
525 Canterbury Road
London, Ontario
Canada N6G 2N5
pendas@pennkemp.ca   pennkemp.ca

The Night the Ducks Got Loose

Charles Mountford

Pendas Poets Series # 16

To John:
I hope you enjoy
this book.

2008

Pendas Productions
London, Ontario, Canada

Dedication

This book is dedicated to
my wife, Ruth,
for her patient advice during the process.

Acknowledgements

Charles Mountford's poetry has appeared in the following publications:

Quarry, Prism International, Lamia Ink (New York — The Poets Theatre Issue published to coincide with the Poets Theatre Festival at La MaMa E.T.C. and Saint Mark's Poetry Project Theatre ReGenesis), *Twenty Cents Magazine*, and *The New Quarterly.*

He has been anthologized in *The Alberta Poetry Year Book, An anthology of London Poets*, and *Here Is A Poem; An anthology of Canadian Poetry.*

His poems, *Lyla, The Rorschach Elephant, The Teeth Of Tarpon Springs, Secret Lover* and *Rain Falls On The Gas Pumps* were performed at The Ripple Effect (The International Augusto Boal Theatre Festival) in Toronto, by the poet.

Charles Mountford is also the author of a previous book of poetry from Pendas Publications called *The Harvestman.*

Charles Mountford writes: "I continue to be grateful to my wife, Ruth, for her wonderful contributions to the design of the book and her great patience while the project was being completed."

A compact disc of Mr. Mountford performing some of his poems, entitled *On My Own*, is available from Pendas Productions.

Preface

I try to write stories, of all kinds, when I write poems. I am happy to exist within the narrative tradition, a tradition which goes all the way back, so they say, to winter nights around the campfire in the cave. Also, I don't see my poems as existing independently. I see them as elements of a big story which I seem to have been telling to myself, and others, since I was a kid and which I hope to continue to tell.

I want my poems to be friendly and accessible but, at the same time, to mean something maybe a little bit more than they seem to at first glance. Also, if I can make the reader smile, a little bit, at some of them it would please me no end.

I hope you enjoy reading these poems as much as I enjoyed writing them.

Charles Mountford
Stratford, 2004

Introduction

We haven't seen poetry like this in Canada since the 1950s. After modernism and post-modernism blew over the country like American oil companies, and after arctic listening stations (again American) eavesdropping on the Russians who were, ostensibly, eavesdropping on us, Charles Mountford has written poetry for people who are still sitting quietly in old brick apartments with torturous plumbing, or in back yards full of cardinals and yellow sunlight, reading Books in Canada in the afternoon and thinking, deeply, from the luxuries of place. These are confident poems, without any wavering or unsurety of identity, yet with ironies so subtle they seem like snow blowing across an August window. Mountford's poem "Polar Bears," for example, opens with "The polar bears burst like bombs/from below the ice," and closes with a sheet of ice sliding overhead to seal us below: "We cannot explain our joy/to see them as they are." It echoes Purdy in the best sense — honouring a tradition, making it personal, and recreating it anew. It is no accident that Mountford is a researcher and restorer of old buildings.

Mountford, however, is not a restorer of Tom Thomson's Canada of flecks of paint imitating maple leaves but of the lives people lived within Canada during its most confident decades. Glenn Gould would have kept this book out at the cottage. The poems in it are like listening to Frank Sinatra croon out song lyrics by Northrop Frye. This is not a spurious comparison: the book is flush with crooners, and the band, in their starry glitter, playing "a solid four beats to every bar//very soft and very, very slow." It's delicious. Like Sinatra, Mountford's sense of self is strong, and, like Sinatra, he constantly undercuts it with a wry taste of tobacco, the breath carefully drawn and savoured. It is savoured, because it is all on stage, from the lounge lizard set piece of "Donny has liquid eyes and all the girls/would like to drink him in," to the hilarious monologue of "Playin' it for Candy." You could make an afternoon program on the CBC out of these pieces. People could set their old bakelite radios on window ledges in old houses shaded with sugar maples, with the gentle rush of an old millrace coming in the window, and would enter the martini hour refreshed and renewed.

As for Northrop Frye, the Frye here is not the Frye of arcane symbolism, ensconced in the crusty Victorian architecture of the University of Toronto, but the Frye of careful attention wrapped up in layer after layer of tissue paper for the delight not of the gift but of its disrobing. Mountford's poetry doesn't always lead us perfectly across the floor, because sometimes we are meant to lead the dance and Mountford is trying to follow, but when he leads, in about half the poems here, we whirl along with him, energized and charmed. These are not big poems. They are not trying to listen to Russia, for instance, but they are, at their best, exquisite, unexpected, populist gems. A hundred small books like this would be good for Canadian poetry. Canadians could make their way home through the storm, arm in arm, shoulder on shoulder, and the rest would be up to them.

Harold Rhenisch
League of Canadian Poets' Communications Committee Chairman
& publisher of The Milestones Review, *a book review quarterly*

Contents

Part 4

Part 5

Part 6

Part 1

The Night the Ducks Got Loose

Millie and Tom were having a romance. She was 73, give or take a few years, and he was 68 and looked it. So, she was seeing a younger man. Just the way it said she should in New Woman Magazine. She didn't care if, being a younger man, he didn't know who he was yet. What she was looking for was passion. And a cup of tea and some raisin squares later.

There hadn't been much passion in her family growing up. Her mother was always a bit cranky because her father's main passion was for ducks, of which he had a herd. It got to the point where he had to buy a border collie to look after them. They were tougher to manage than sheep.

It had been humiliating when her own husband had left her for a much younger woman, a child really, of 35, named Silky whose body was pierced in an embarrassingly large number of places. She was blonde and pouty and Millie knew she'd run to fat.

Millie was worried that Carl, her husband, wouldn't like it after a while and would fret and not have clean socks. Then she met Tom and it didn't seem to matter so much any more.

Tonight she was happy. Blissful, even. She'd won at bingo. Her husband, Carl, looking old, had sat with her just like in the old days, elbow to elbow, and she'd found out that Silky had left him for a man who owned a tattoo parlour and was now tattooed where she wasn't pierced. Also, she was now fat, as Millie had always known she would be.

After a good talk and after Carl bought her a cup of coffee, she went back home to Tom and now she was dreaming she was back on the farm down by the fenced in duck pond. The ducks were pressed against the gate like a snow drift and a border collie with human hands was gently disentangling them and letting them out of the gate, one by one, to the delicious freedom of the meadow.

Tom stirred in his sleep and his hand touched hers.

"You are my good shepherd." she said, aloud, without waking and without waking him.

The Centre of the Universe

I woke up, feeling rested and content,
just after lunch on a Saturday afternoon
in February with the snow piled firewood high

outside the windows. I walked into
the livingroom taking it for granted,
Lord knows why, that I was the centre

of the universe. None of you have ever
done that, I'm sure. But I did.
And my wife, bless her, looked over at me

and smiled and my dog yawned
and I suddenly knew. They wanted
the centre of the universe to get outside right now

and shovel off the sidewalk
and scrape the windows of the car clean
and warm it up so that they

could drive downtown and drive a hard bargain or two
with all the other centres of the universe
who worked down there.

Worried About Love

Eunice and Clarkie live in a trailer at the edge of town, right next to the gravel road that goes, eventually, to Port Rose, the next town down the lake.

Every February, after a couple of weeks of being snowed in so bad they can hardly get out the door for five minutes, she starts hallucinating that he doesn't love her any more.

She sits in the kitchen window, crammed in between the table and the sharp edges of the cupboard, looks out at the blowing snow and cries. Great, man-killing sobs that come from some endless, uncharted ocean of grief centred on broken promises, lost dreams, earrings she only has one of now, an old dog they had that got run over by a pulp truck one day and a vague memory of her father who died when she was three, she thinks.

Her father was perfect. He would never take a drink, she blurts out, blubbering. He would keep the snow shovelled. He lived in a house not in some ratty little trailer almost falls apart every time the wind blows, and so on. And on and on.

Clarkie doesn't mind. He loves her. Yes, he does. No, he's not lying and if she doesn't believe him he'll take off all his clothes right now and go out in the snow for a little hike and freeze to death and maybe then she'll believe him for once.

He has his shirt off, not an inspiring sight, by the time he finishes saying this and is starting on his pants when she stops him by handing him a cup of coffee, that has been well watered with her tears. Of course, the smell of coffee is to Clarkie like the smell of new shoes to Eunice. It stops him cold. No matter what he's doing he just has to have that coffee.

Eunice knows this. After fifteen years of marriage, she's a walking encyclopedia of what stops Clarkie cold.

So there's a temporary truce. They sit and drink coffee side by side, breathing together, in rhythm. It feels warmer in the trailer. Maybe tomorrow there will be a thaw.

Superfrown

I am learning how to frown.
Is it a bird? Is it a dinosaur?
Is it a man? No. It's superfrown.

Thus do we become our heroes.
Our frowning fathers. Our frowning grandfathers.
Our frowning aunts, uncles, brothers, sisters, cousins.

Frown upon frown. Upon frown.
And, in the fullness of time,
the usual reward of frown.

We become the boss. We sit
in the frowning office. High up.
We now have the ultimate choice.

So, we surround ourselves with smiles.
A grey, burnt place surrounded by tulips.

Damned Nice

I hope for some success,
some love, some, may I say it,
money? Some hiccup in the natural laws

that leads me a few steps
in the direction of the tower of ambition.
That would be nice. Or, if the word nice

doesn't suit you, very nice or, depending
on your personality, damned nice,
for a change. Damned nice,

I might shout out, in front of my
mirror, in my bathroom, early
in my morning, shaving.

And it would be, for me.
Sort of like seeing an orange bird,
an oriole, say, in a certain light,

or having Roger Federer whisper
a few tennis secrets to me alone
just before a big game at the club.

That kind of damned nice.

Blue

Dahlia, from childhood, had always liked the colour blue but it wasn't until she was fifty, with the children more or less out on their own and the grandchildren showing up only about once a week or so (Dahlia said she'd like them more but her daughter, Sandi, knew better from long experience and limited the visits), it was only then that she had time to "go in" for blue.

First off, when things really started getting serious, she and Fred bought a blue Chevy. Fred was willing to go that far, no problem. He didn't mind when she painted the house blue, either. Inside and out, with blue carpets, blue refrigerator and stove, blue glass in all the windows, blue dishes. Knives and forks, ditto. Also, washer and dryer.

She got a blue rinse, too, which he didn't lose any sleep over. That seemed normal at her age. Nothing wrong with that.

Blue clothes, blue underwear, blue sheets, towels and pillow cases. Blue soap, blue food, blue coffee. Everything blue. No problem.

As he said to the guys in the back booth of the Myrtle Beach Café (four skinny old guys in plaid caps, rayon pants, golf jackets and bolo ties with moosehead clasps that the Legion gave out free last Christmas), "It's up to her. She's always used her head. If you can't trust your wife, who can you trust?"

But, he drew the line when she spray painted the dog and the cat blue. Who needed something like that? And he drew the line even deeper when she came down for breakfast, one morning, stark naked and painted blue. Blue. In this kind of weather. At her age. It was enough to make a man forget about breakfast. He couldn't get out of the house fast enough.

Then he was afraid to go home. He figured he was next. She'd probably paint him blue when he was asleep and he'd wake up and wonder where he was and all he'd be able to see would be these huge blue toes at the end of the couch and beyond them his wife, grinning, with her new blue teeth.

All this dress-up stuff was OK for her but who needed a new blue fire chief? That was the kind of thing that made his men a little bit uneasy. Red they could handle and yellow, too. But blue? He just didn't know.

The mayor was no help. He said, "Who knows? Women do funny things at a certain age. Maybe that's what this is."

His son, the big dummy, just laughed and told him it was an opportunity for growth. He wondered how much growth there would be if she started in on the grandchildren next. That might be really worth the wait.

A Rainbow of the Streets

Twyla ran across my street, clickety click,
in her eight inch spike heels, red shoes rocking.

"Seeing that man again." the flower-seller's wife
remarked. Not to me. What did she care about me?
I was just a transaction, not the real action.

Twyla hopped on one foot, gave a red-lipped shout
as she dropped her bag but the bus driver,
so gallant you couldn't believe, swerved
at the last minute and Twyla, bag intact,

head unbowed, walked like a red-headed
empress up the sagging steps and through
the green doorway. I could distinctly hear
her boy friend suck back his breath as she

walked up ten long flights of stairs,
no trouble at all, and he still held his breath
as her key fumbled in the door of his room

and then I heard him shout as he
let it all out the moment she slammed
the door behind her and stood, lit by the sun
from his window, a rainbow of the streets.

Secret Lover

Every woman needs a secret lover. To be good to her when things are not going very good.

Marie's secret lover was Elvis. Nothing strange about that. Everybody knew he was the secret lover of half the women in town. The other half had either Tom Jones or Engelbert. We're talking women here, mind. Who knew what the kids wanted? Who wanted to know, for that matter? That was a whole different pierced nose, bright blue-haired line of thought going on.

Marie had it bad. She was President of the ESL (Elvis Secret Lover), fan club. Everybody in the club had the house set up on an Elvis theme. There was Elvis wallpaper, sheets and blankets. Elvis hand towels in the bathroom. Elvis plates to eat off of. An Elvis water dish for the dog.

The husbands didn't mind. They all liked Elvis. Maybe not as much as John Wayne, The Duke, but he was right up there.

Marie even invented a pie in the shape of Elvis but when it was all done it looked so darn wonderful she just couldn't bring herself to eat any of it. So she fed it to her husband, Ricky and Ricky ate the whole thing in one sitting. He loved it. So much so that he got her to make one every Thursday night and he'd take a piece (maybe one of Elvis' legs or an arm), to work and eat it while he was drinking his coffee, which had been poured from his Elvis thermos into his Elvis cup.

Of all the guys in town, Marie thought that Ricky looked the most like Elvis, once she'd got through making him over. He looked particularly good (and all the other women just had to agree, it was so true), in the white jump suit and the cape. All he needed now was a big, white limo with mink upholstery and she was saving for that out of her house money. She figured at the rate she was going they'd have the limo in about two hundred years or so and then they could all drive down to Graceland and pay their respects in style.

For Marie, Elvis came to her at night, usually after she'd eaten a bit too much tuna casserole. After he sang a couple of numbers, just for her, they sat down, she and Elvis, and had a cup of coffee and talked, just like old friends. It was all so sweet she figured she must have died and gone to Heaven.

She couldn't believe Elvis was so wise. The advice he gave her was so right on the mark. He told her, mostly, good things, like where to get bargains and what numbers to play at bingo on Friday nights. He also told her to be good to Ricky, to feed him right, to keep him in shape and to make sure his head stayed on straight. Don't fight with him, Elvis made her promise.

Marie did everything Elvis told her to do. Exactly. So she had a wonderful marriage. And, as for Ricky, the lucky guy, he didn't even know why.

The Missing Link

The missing link is in my dreams.
Strong, resourceful, a survivor.
He climbs, sturdily, over rocks
and crosses the dry plains
of prehistory with a dogged gait.

I don't know where he lives
or if his mortgage is more
than he can handle
or if his wife and children
are as frightened as I am
of his stone axe and his laser rifle.

He seems friendly enough.
Guileless, even. A friendly smile
and a firm handshake
that would have fooled me, once.
But now I have had enough of innocence.
I need to hold his guilt

in my own guilty hands.

Thanksgiving

LaVerne was a deeply spiritual woman who always went to church in extremely short skirts on the theory that God might enjoy looking at her legs and, since He was all-powerful, who had more right?

Certainly not her husband, Claude, who hadn't seen LaVerne without her clothes on since their first date when she had been wild and wonderful beyond any of his expectations. He had married her on the strength of those expectations, not knowing how truly spiritual she was, and was now paying the price. He was a hard-headed businessman but even the hardest head turns to mush when it's a matter of love.

Their daughter, Ruby, was going to be having a birthday on Saturday, nothing special, just family and her boyfriend, Franks. Claude considered Franks an idiot and had no intention of giving him a soft, well-paying job in his business, no matter how hard Ruby pleaded his case. Claude and Ruby were on a real collision course, here, two major freight trains heading for a head-on crash, with Franks right in the middle.

Franks didn't care. He was one of those guys who figure if there's a crash there's always going to be someone else around to sweep the road and pick up the pieces. He knew that Ruby was a good thing as far as he was concerned. All he had to do was to figure a way to get her father out of the picture.

LaVerne liked Franks. Naturally. It figured she would, right? She knew that he could really care and be deeply saved if he just thought about it for a minute. Maybe, she figured, Ruby could start him thinking about his spirituality and reaching for a higher plane of things. After all, she'd given him lots to think about already.

LaVerne was studying and praying on how to make this happen.

Franks wasn't averse to being spiritual if it meant he got Ruby. See, he had this dream where he was escorting Ruby, both of them dressed to the hilt, naturally, to all of these high-level functions, such as the annual Thanksgiving dance at the country club, where he could mingle with some of the top guns in town and cut a fine figure for once. That would show his mother. She'd always said he'd never amount to much but it stood to reason she could have made a mistake. She wasn't perfect, was she? After all, she had married his father.

Claude, however, expected to spend Thanksgiving giving thanks that Franks was gone. Plain out-of-sight gone. He promised himself that he'd donate a new hole to the country club if this happened.

But God works in mysterious ways. Claude had a heart attack, a big one, two days before Thanksgiving at his girlfriend, Wanda's, plush, hideaway apartment just as Franks was picking him up in the Oldsmobile. Franks explained everything to LaVerne and Ruby in such an inventive, amusing, clear and doggone low-down spiritual way that Claude, instead of being the goat, became a fallen hero in the eyes of his family. He realized, in a flash of blinding clarity, that maybe Franks was cut out to be a businessman after all. He certainly had at least one of the main talents needed for the job.

So Ruby is happy now and so is LaVerne. Claude is still recovering in the hospital but now he's got Franks to look after things, so why should he worry?

Wanda didn't send flowers, which was thoughtful of her, in more ways than one. However, she did phone and tell him that she'd bought a new nightie for when he was up to it again, as she put it.

So, Thanksgiving wasn't a complete bust. There was, after all, lots to be thankful for.

Part 2

The Price of Heaven

It's been a winter full of snow this year.

Eddie Glocken, a high school teacher in Port Rose who lives in Shaking Bay (he'll take Port Rose money but damned if he'll live there), has had to drive through it every morning to work. And back every night.

Through the damned snow.

Twenty-five miles each way on a country road that catches the wind just perfect so that it's not only snowing, it's blowing so hard you can hardly see ten feet in front of yourself. It's like driving through a bowl of milk.

So, when the school board decided, in a rare fit of common sense, to offer early retirement to old crocks in their fifties like him he jumped at the chance. He had visions of himself and his wife, Doris, who worked answering the phone for Beet Springstone, the dentist, gallivanting about at the golf club all summer and being cool and sophisticated at the curling club all winter, just like the doctors and lawyers up on Hill Street.

Of course, the doctors and lawyers had to work full out into their eighties, nobody was offering them an early retirement package but, hey, you can't have everything. Eddie liked that idea.

Doris said it was OK with her. She said she liked golf. She even said she liked curling.

So the deed was done and, by the end of June, he was free. Free. For the first time in his life. Not a worry in the world and a decent income without working. For life.

Things couldn't get much better.

On July 2, Doris was shelling peas over the sink. She had a thoughtful expression on her face. He stopped, on his way through the kitchen, struck by her expression.

"What's up?" he said.

"Well," she said, slowly, "Mom's not going to live forever, you know."

"Oh, yeah," he agreed, although he figured she might.

"And," she said, in a rush, "now that you're here full time like you are, I want to quit my job and bring her home to live with us. Then I can look after her myself. She's never been happy at The Residence."

What could he do? He was trapped and he knew it. Heaven had a price after all.

The old lady wasn't any more trouble than any other old lady in her eighties who was just gathering enough steam to head full throttle down the hill to dementia. Also, she had a major cigarette habit that she didn't want, in this life, ever to overcome. In fact, she was delighted to succumb to it. Which was OK except for the fact that she burned holes in everything with her cigarettes and, one afternoon, had to be rescued when she lit her chair on fire while watching television.

He smelled smoke and came into the room and there she was, surrounded by a thick fog, smiling and dabbing gently at a big, burned spot on the chair with a Kleenex.

So, he and Doris had words and, since Doris had more words than he did, she won. So her mother stayed. And stayed.

It wasn't what he'd pictured when he signed the papers to retire. He'd thought more in terms of himself, looking ten years younger, at the controls of a red Piper Cub. Something like that. Now it seemed he'd never get out of the hangar.

Of course, it didn't help when all the guys down at the beer parlour brought out mother-in-law stories, which, to be fair, made his own situation seem wonderful by comparison.

Not that he could see it that way. They were just guys. Ordinary guys had their problems. Everybody knew that. But it didn't seem fair that he should have trouble. It shouldn't happen like that. He was different. He was from somewhere else. Not from Earth, maybe. Maybe from Mars. That was probably it.

The good thing was, Doris was happy. Who could knock that? She looked more than ten years younger.

Another good thing was that Time, while it's a crock that it's a great healer, at least gave you a chance to get used to anything.

This being true, eventually there came a day when he turned to Doris and said, "You know, I love our life." And meant it.

So, he was in Heaven after all. A smoky kind of Heaven that they had somehow neglected to mention in church.

Part 3

What the afterlife might be like for those who can't quite make up their minds what to believe in

I wonder what the afterlife is like
for those who can't make up their minds
what they believe in. Do they wander?
Or is it more like a gigantic Home Depot

where they go from bin to bin
picking up the bolts of one belief,
the super glue of another, the plastic pipe
of a third and, then, when they reach

the check out counter, just before
the endlessly patient woman asks
for their spiritual debit cards,
they decide, oh no, this isn't it

and take the cart back and unpack it —
into the wrong bins — and start again,
choosing another aisle for eternity,
one that looks longer and more exciting.

Elephants on Broadway

Lyla's cousin, Lester, was in Manhattan again last Fall. When he was there he got a sudden urge for an elephant. It happened just when he was sitting in this delicatessen on Broadway eyeing a secretary, skinny as a twig, who was chomping her way through about ten pounds of prosciutto ham with melon on the side.

Now, most places don't do elephants. New York does. If you've got the money. So, he phones a guy. The guy says, "An elephant? Sure. What's the address? Is that so? Say, is my secretary in there? Skinny, big mop of sand-coloured hair? Glasses?"

"Does she like prosciutto?" Lester asks.

"Yeah. Eats about ten pounds every lunch. Is that a tapeworm or what?"

"Yeah," Lester says. "she's here."

"Well, put her on for a few minutes, will you?"

Lester motions to the woman with the melon on the side, who immediately assumes that he's a sex maniac or, even worse, a tourist and ignores him. He tells this to the guy on the phone.

"Her name's Gloria" the guy says, meanwhile shouting at what sounds like a revolutionary mob in the background. "Also, she's kind of deaf. So you have to speak up. Can you do it?"

Lester turns around. Gloria is still ignoring him in favour of three loaves of banana bread.

"Gloria!" he shouts. "It's your boss! He wants to talk!"

"What are you shouting for?" she says, reaching for the phone and putting it close to her lips in a delicate way as if she was kissing a strawberry mousse. "I ain't deaf."

She and her boss talk for maybe ten minutes. Finally, she hangs up the phone.

"Five minutes" she says, in a loud voice. She looks around the deli. "Guy here wants an elephant" she says to everybody, pointing her thumb at Lester and making it sound as though he was a mysterious sexual commodity that had just come onto the market.

Two or three people stand up to have a better look at him. One of them is an old lady who's been worrying a macaroon to death for at least half an hour with what remains of her teeth.

"Is that so?" she says. "My brother-in-law tried an elephant once. He hurt his back."

There are expressions of sympathy for her brother-in-law all over the deli. They look at Lester as though he is responsible for the brother-in-law's miserable life.

Gloria snaps her purse shut and squeezes her lips together into a tight circle.

"Five minutes" she says. "Out front."

Lester goes out front. Down Broadway comes a cab hauling a contraption with, sure enough, an elephant on it. It stops in front of the deli. The elephant steps down onto the street, delicately. It stands looking at him, obviously expecting him to pay for the cab. Now, as a rule, he doesn't pay for cabs taken by elephants. But there are exceptions.

Half of the deli has come out onto the sidewalk with him. The old lady says to the elephant, "You poor dear. I know what you'll go through."

Lester is starting to feel publicly exposed. He says to the cab driver, "The elephant and I will take a turn around the park. Maybe even rent a cabriolet."

The cab driver looks at him in amazement. He says, "Not in this cab you won't. I got standards, you know. Take a walk, fella. You and your elephant."

There are mutters of agreement from the crowd on the sidewalk. Lester can see he is anti-elephant. Absolutely. It's just his luck to draw a cabbie with a closed mind.

"Look" Lester says, "if it makes you feel any better, I'm a research scientist. The elephant is an experiment. We're going to the U.N. building to test the effect of elephants on elevators."

He has to say something. It makes the driver less suspicious about what he is up to.

"That's different." the cabbie says. "I thought you said the park."

You can see he's made trips to the U.N. building with an elephant before. Cab drivers in New York see everything.

As Lester leaves the deli, sitting in the front seat — the elephant has the back — the old lady pokes her umbrella at him.

"You treat her like a lady, now" she says. "I've got the number of this cab. There'll be trouble if you don't."

Is It My Fault the Sun Did That?

The sun, wearing a cool, summer suit,
dark glasses and a panama hat
and carrying a fancy bamboo walking stick

looking, in fact, a lot like my Uncle Frank,
except a little more red in the face
and with a somewhat louder voice,

came down out of the sky
and sat with me at a little
table in a far corner of my garden.

He wanted to sit in the grape
arbour but I steered him
out into the open

as far away from the plants
as I could but, even then,
I could see he was having

an unfortunate effect.
He left a big hole in the sky, too,
which upset the neighbours.

I could see them talking
and I knew I'd be blamed,
particularly if I kept him too much to myself

and didn't introduce him around.
But what could I do?
He was calling the shots.

As I said later, who knew?
Was it my fault a major player
like that dropped in?

Radio

There's a cold night hovering over the neighbourhood, like a big, snowy owl. It hasn't quite landed yet but everybody knows it's coming. GBNR radio, the Voice of the Bay Area, has been scaring the daylights out of everybody over sixty years old all afternoon by reminding them every fifteen minutes how easy it is to freeze to death when you're past a certain age.

Beet Springstone, the dentist, and his parents left for Florida on Beet's private jet around noon. They'll be in Tarpon Springs in an hour or so and the radio down there will be scaring his parents to death all holiday by reminding them every fifteen minutes about heat prostration, sunstroke, the dangers of over-exertion and too frequent sex after a flight from a colder climate. They'll live in air conditioning all winter parked in front of a big colour television set in the family condo while Beet does some volunteer work on a Lufthansa stewardess he met at the airport.

Connie

Connie, Lyla the hairdresser's kid sister, is not going to Florida this winter or any other winter. She's going somewhere, though. She just decided. See, her boyfriend, Thad, walked out on her without any warning last night. Oh, he was coming back even though he said he wasn't. She still had hopes, etc. and etc.

Connie is the one who has that little apartment in town, the one with the Christmas wrapping paper pasted all over the windows and Bing Crosby singing White Christmas on the stereo all day. The mood she's in she may never come out of her apartment again. Just her and Bing. Together for life.

Eventually, however, she relented, as we all do, and decided to give life another chance. She bought a ticket to Hollywood, on the bus. She got a job down there, at an Orange Julius, serving, under a big blow-up poster of Gary Cooper, orange juice to the stars. She wished Thad could see her with Gary. That would make him think. He'd pause, then, she figured.

Once, she thought she saw Thad looking at her through the window. It made her happy, even if he didn't come in, because he looked lost. It reminded her of Reverend Passlake's Christmas sermon back home, that she sat through just before she left, on the topic of how the lost shall be found. She truly hoped that her lost (meaning Thad), could be found.

And then thoroughly dumped.

.

The Sea Horse

In the swimming pool
I am some new species
of sea horse

a snorting, puffing kind
that knows some Latin
and less Greek

that has read the Bible
and forgotten most of it
except the scary parts

the kind that takes his flippers off
when he reads the newspaper
and laughs at the comics

who enjoys himself hugely
in his chlorine scented sea
but stretches most contentedly

in his native sun
under a blue sky
and breathes in air

through a large, burned
landlubber nose.

What We Don't Know About Betty

What makes Betty Betty? Quite frankly, we don't know. We care, oh yes, we care a lot. But caring and knowing? And knowing to care? Well...

We see her. Not too tall. Slightly more than a little plump. What could be a worried expression on her face. Not that we're saying she's worried, mind you. Lordy, no. We just don't know.

And that corner where she is standing. Could that be a bus stop? It looks like a bus stop. Buses stop there. But that could be by accident.

Every time a bus stops Betty looks up timidly and begins, it seems, to move and we say, "Yes! Go get him girl!" because the bus driver, a bearded giant in overalls and a uniform cap, has his arms open wide welcoming Betty aboard his bus. We don't go in much for lip reading but any fool could guess what he is saying. He is saying, in a deep, manly, yet non-threatening and certainly not overtly sexist way, "Yes. This is my bus. Come aboard. Everyone is welcome. This is bus country. Only exact change, please."

But Betty never gets on the bus. Maybe she doesn't have the exact change. This is possible. We just don't know. How long will she have to stand there? Until she does have exact change? We don't know that either.

All that we do know is that she is Betty.

Someone must feed Betty and clothe her and see that she has baths. We don't know who this could be. Is it the tall man with the serious look on his face and exact change in his right hand that he keeps counting over and over and over with increasing anxiety to make sure that it stays exact? Who knows? Is it the young boy with the high powered target rifle in the leather carrying case that he hopes no one will notice? We don't know what to think.

Once, a fight broke out on the corner where Betty is standing. A tall man with weak ankles, a walking stick and spats began to wrestle with a fat man in an informal costume of some kind. Were they fighting about Betty? Betty isn't going to tell us. I don't think she even noticed them. But I don't know that.

And that sweet little girl with the stuffed animal. Is that Betty's daughter? She's as much a puzzle as Betty.

Every day we see Betty and the little girl standing at the same corner while people walk past who seem to ignore them, seem to be totally unconcerned but all the time are wondering, in a mood between fear and anger, what makes Betty Betty?

We just don't know.

Part 4

Why I Miss Her So Much

The sun wafts an "I am morning"
hue over the roof of my garage
and over the last of the carrots
in my fall garden.

Summer, with her legs
and blonde hair, her loose dresses
and her bare feet, will no longer
sit with me under the vine-covered

pergola nor will I hear the music
of her walkman, a jazz quintet
featuring an amazing, but little known,
trumpet player whom, I imagine,

she has left town to meet
and with whom she will spend
her vacation in some lucky spot
with the word "palm" in its name.

In any case, she has left
her flowered hat behind,
a careless promise to return,
and a phone number to call

if I ever need to remember
why I miss her so much.

Doc Brainerd In Focus

For years, Doc Brainerd insisted that there was something moving, there, right there, almost got it in focus that time, right in the extreme corner of his vision. He said that he thought it was his mother trying to contact him from the spirit world where she's been living for twenty-five years now. However, he wasn't sure because, whatever it was, it kept sliding away no matter how quickly he turned his head.

His mother was very important to him. He lived with her all his life, through medical school, two years in the Korean War (they shared a tent that time) and then back home to a GP's life in the big house on India Street, full of the gadgets and shepherdesses in china that she bought with the money he gave her.

When she died he was broken up, of course, but he needed somebody to dust that china so he married, about a year later, an active widow named Corinne, a woman who'd been dreaming of a doctor in her life all her life but, because of circumstances beyond her control, had settled for a succession of long-haul truckers.

Corinne understood about his mother. She was a woman of great understanding. When he complained that his mother was restless where she was living now because she needed a cup of cocoa which, all her life, she'd had at this time of the day, Corinne would get up without a word and make a cup for her and the Doc and they'd sit drinking it, the Doc explaining that the essence of the drink somehow, he was sure, found its way into the spirit world and how kind and understanding Corinne was to know this. Corinne just nodded. Spend your life married to long-haul truckers and you begin to understand a lot of things.

Corinne kept up her contacts with the trucking industry and every so often she'd hitch a ride on somebody's rig to Vancouver. "Haul ass to the coast," as she put it. She'd stay away anywheres up to a month and come back refreshed and ready for anything the Doc could throw at her.

And so it happened that, one evening about five years into their marriage, the Doc and Corinne were having cocoa together and watching Letterman on TV when all of a sudden he said, in a fairly loud voice, "Mother. So it is you. Look, Corinne." Then he slumped on the couch and died. He had finally got his life into focus just as it left him.

Corinne called the ambulance and sat there holding his hand and drinking cocoa, waving her cup around, sharing with his mother as always, until the men came. And, as she waited, it seemed to her that there was something moving, there, right there, almost got it in focus that time, right in the extreme corner of her vision.

I Miss My Father

I look out the back window
and see my father digging.

I look out the front window
and see my father mowing the lawn.

He comes in the back door.
The front door opens and there he stands.

When I stand at the back window
I stand the way he stood.

When I am outside, he
is inside painting a room.

When I want to talk to him
he has just left.

I hear his car every day
pulling into the driveway,

the engine ticking cold,
the car door slamming.

Whenever I see my father
around the house, I miss him.

The Gamecock

When I entered the cool of the barn
the rooster skittered in after me.

So light and graceful he moved,
with such a sure and deadly purpose.

One would have thought my size
precluded his hope to make his bones.

However, perhaps he saw my face,
towering above him, as the moon

and yearned to sink his spurs
into those distant, lonely, eye sockets.

Sondra Will Get Married

A fair number of men around here tend to approach women with the same caution that they use when they go out on the lake in a thunderstorm. They do it only when they really have to and, when they do, they make it a short trip and they sit as low as they can in the boat.

For these men, it follows that marriage is a dangerous, mysterious and who knows what could happen state best left to women. When they do, finally, get married they try to pretend that it has happened to somebody else. This pretend state can, and frequently does, last for years.

Snell Jutland, for example, a married man with three grown children, died last week without a will. He didn't feel a will was necessary in his case. He figured that some other guy named Snell Jutland had married his wife and fathered his children and it was this guy who needed a will. That was obvious. Any fool knew that. But why would he want one?

This afternoon, a delightful Saturday in June, Margaret and Ted Mention's determined daughter, Sondra, is standing waiting in the church in her wedding dress, a dress that used to belong to her grandmother. This is the same dress that her mother wore when she got married and the same dress that her father spilled coffee on just before this afternoon's wedding. He's been banished to the car until the exact moment when he has to take her down the aisle. Hopefully, he'll be finished his coffee by then.

If he's not, Sondra's brother, Toddo, will gently take the coffee out of his hands. And then spill it on one of the bridesmaids.

Sondra continues to smile. The boat continues to head out into the lake. The men sit lower than ever before. Marriage continues to remain mysterious to them all.

The Outdoor Experience

I wish I was one
of those early ones
who could hunt, without guilt,

all the songbirds of America
but I can't, their ghosts
hang too heavy in the sky

knowing what once was
and can never be again.
I sit in my lawn chair

sipping lemonade with
a Nature CD pouring
thrush songs and the rattle

of water over pebbles,
now and then adjusting
my headphones to maximize

the outdoor experience.

Vacation Music

I am walking in the shallow water
near the beach, in lime green bermuda
shorts and hand-painted hawaiian shirt,
a cocoa straw hat pushed back on my head
and my heart full of island music

so that out of my mouth the notes
of a ukelele fall like silver keys
and my vacation puddles at my feet
like my city clothes, tossed
into the hotel closet in a heap.

I Miss You Miss Country and Western

I sit in the back rooms
of my heart missing you, or
someone awfully like you.

I sing, over and over again,
the first few lines of some
country and western song while

my hat fills with rain,
my shoes warp and I spend
nothing but money worrying

when you might come back
and hoping against hope that,
in the end, you might not,

while the room revolves around me
like a bad bridging chorus
and an even worse last verse.

Part 5

The Swan Dive

"Tube" Tubeling's wife, the former Nancy Jean Wryzowski, died of a psychosomatic illness brought on suddenly by a fall from the balcony of the fourteenth floor of an apartment building.

She landed on the roof of a taxi that had just offloaded The Magnificent Sandra, Queen of the Exotics, 300 lbs. of thrill & chill, who was visiting her ex-husband, a Certified General Accountant by the name of Eddie, in the building, to "choke some more support money out of the little bastard," as she put it.

The former Nancy Jean Wryzkowski's unfortunate accident caused The Magnificent Sandra to forget why she was there in the first place for at least eight seconds and severely discomfited the taxi driver, newly arrived from Kowloon Forbidden City and convinced beyond any hope of redemption that he had brought the incident on himself by failing to approach the building from the proper direction for starters and by neglecting to have his horoscope done before the trip.

He froze instantly into trauma, totally convinced that he now inhabited a cursed life and that the sky would continue to rain women down upon the roof of his taxicab until he managed to find the correct charms to ease the anger of whatever powerful forces he had obviously offended.

The doorman, an ex-wrestler by the name of Mickey, shared his viewpoint, as was indicated by his one comment which was, "Shit. A swan dive. And on my shift, yet."

I Know You

I am one of those people
that you see alone in a room
at night with the window open

and the light unabashedly on
sitting at a table or a desk,
a pen and some blank paper

nearby, who, when you jog by
in your shorts, intent on fitness,
notices you without turning his head

and sends an almost invisible hive
of buzzing bees after you down the street
and may later write your name

on a page calling you a tree
or some animal name that rhymes
with the line before, some name

that only you have ever called
yourself and, even then, in secret.
I am one of those people.

Bert Delivers

In town, you should go to the store yourself. This is good advice that any local will give you. It's much faster than waiting for Bert, the delivery boy, who's eighty years old and half the time forgets and takes your order home for himself.

Bert lives at home with his parents. They always call him "the boy" as in, "The boy's around here somewheres." He gets twenty-five cents a delivery from the U Got It Rite We Sell Everything Store, where he's been working for the last seventy-five years. It doesn't seem like much but what with tips and his allowance from his parents he does O.K.

Since he lives at home, he doesn't have much in the way of expenses and, as a boy, he doesn't have many bad habits, yet. In fact, if the truth were known and, believe me, it is, he's worth eighteen million dollars, give or take a million dollars or so, depending on who is doing the addition down at the combination bank and sawmill that day.

Bert now spends the colder months in Palm Beach. He goes down in a stretch limo. Hates flying. His bicycle and his girlfriend, Bobbi Lee, eighteen years old and with really big hair, go with him.

Down in the Palm, the locals know him as Mr. B. Rumours abound about the source of his wealth, most agreeing that it's probably old money. This, if you know anything about the spending habits of the people in town, is not really that bad of a guess. Very old would be better.

Imagine How My Dog Felt

Imagine how my dog felt
when I wouldn't open
the car window on his side

so that he could stick
his big head out and gulp
air and smile.

Imagine how you would feel
if I stole your favourite sweater
and gave it to my dog

so he would forgive me
for not opening that window
and imagine how I would feel

if you stole my dog
and later I saw you both
in your car on Main Street

his head out the open window
his feet standing
on your favourite sweater

his eyes laughing at me.

Bringing Up Sammy

The son of my proctologist, Bernie, is a sappy kid named Sam. You can tell from looking at him that he's never going to be the man his father is. At least, you can tell if you happen to be Bernie.

Where Bernie waxes, the kid wanes. Bernie has big, hard looking hands and hairy wrists. When he reams you out with the cattle prod he calls a periscope, you stay reamed.

Sam, however, wants to be an artist. He's already produced two or three thousand watercolours, mostly of his mother who happens to be (this is Bernie talking, here), at the root of all his problems.

Not to mention that dopey cat of his, Fluff. Who can believe a cat that wouldn't bite the head off a squirrel if you handed it to him on a silver platter? Between his mother and his cat it's no wonder Sam doesn't know what end is up.

Many times Bernie has tried to take the kid into his office. Show him the business, like. How a real man puts in his eight hours. He even bought him a small, practice periscope but the kid wouldn't even use it on the cat. What kind of kid is that, I ask you?

So, they're at an impasse, Sam and Bernie. It's like two chess masters stonewalling each other. Bernie even published a book, a damned good one, too, called "The Art of Proctology" in which he wrote the captions to a fine selection of art photos of him and his patients going at it.

The book made him a legend in his profession. There wasn't a doctor's office in the country that didn't have at least one of the pictures framed and hanging in a prominent spot.

Of course, Bernie checked with his lawyers to make sure that he wasn't violating confidentiality, here, but they assured him that since you couldn't see faces he wasn't really telling tales out of school, so to speak.

Sam, though, wouldn't even open up the book. Cost a mint to print, too. But, oh, no, not him. Wouldn't touch it. Wouldn't give Bernie the benefit of the doubt at all.

Bernie didn't know what to do. The world was a jungle out there. You had to be a proctologist to survive. Who was going to buy dumb pictures of a little, middle-aged Polish lady with glasses sitting beside an obviously constipated cat?

And wasn't the cat, which appeared in every picture, some sort of attack on Bernie, himself? Didn't the kid know a thing like that could make his father a laughingstock?

But what did they care? They had their paper and their paints. And they had each other.

Bernie couldn't see it. He knew it had to go bad in the end. In his experience, everything eventually did.

Casual and Natural,
I Reach the Top of the Stairs

I felt astonishment
as I reached the top
of the stairs and saw

that there was nothing
there, not even light or dark.
Nothing at the top of the stairs.

And so I stepped into nothingness
a being stepping into non-being,
as casually as a gorilla peels a banana,

as naturally as a flower
drops orange petals
all over your mouth.

John Sobieski, the National Hero of Poland, is resurrected as a chartered accountant in the Twenty-First Century and tries to make it on TV

John Sobieski was a well-known chartered accountant who made his pile in transferables. Money that was transferred to him and, somehow, never transferred past him.

He liked to hang around a place in town called Slopesie's, home of the celebrity look-a-likes and the plastic surgeons who made them that way.

Once he'd made his pile, John had himself surgically altered into a midget President Dwight D. Eisenhower look-a-like at Slopesie's — or, at least, by a guy he met at Slopesie's.

He did this because he'd always wanted to retire into show business and he'd been told by a theatrical agent that he had to carve his niche.

Now, he'd no sooner had this done (in fact, the bandages across his eyes had just been taken off that morning), when in comes a casting assistant into the place on the dead run knocking over two Federico Fellini look-a-likes and a close, but not quite, knock-off of Fabio and shouts:

"Quick! I need three Jimmy Carters. A small one for distance shots, a regular, and a tall one for closeups. Oh, yeah, and a John Sobieski."

Now, you have to understand that whenever this happens it's pandemonium, if not worse, because that's the whole point of the place. Casting.

But you also have to understand the position this puts John in. I mean, there he is, a midget perfect President Eisenhower waiting for a casting call for, like, even a small part would be wonderful and what happens? They need a John Sobieski.

So he loses his mind. "That's me!" he shouts. "Me! I'm John Sobieski!"

The casting assistant looks at a photograph clipped to his wrist. "You don't look like a John Sobieski. He's tall, bald, an accountant. A CGA, even. You're not like him at all." He sneers. "Must have been some makeover you got. Try somebody that knows Sobieski next time."

He moves to get out of there. John grabs his arm. He is babbling. "But it's me. I could be me again. Look, there's my surgeon. He's got me in a can somewhere." He searches for a word. Finds it. His eyes are glazed over. "I could be resurrected!"

John makes a slight motion. Instantly, a plastic surgeon breaks from the pack surrounding a Madonna/Hillary Clinton knock-off and skids into place beside John, leaving scuff marks on Slopesie's carpet, the recipient, if not the victim, of innumerable other encounters of the same kind.

"John!" he says, smiling at the casting assistant. "It's John!"

"He don't look like John," the casting man says, sullenly. His eyes, which had seen it all and then some, flick impatiently around the room.

"But he could be. He could be again," the surgeon says.

"Are you the guy tried to make him look like Sobieski in the first place?" the casting assistant asks. "If you are, you made a hell of a mess." He shows the surgeon the photograph. "That's Sobieski."

"No," the doctor says, frantically. "This is Sobieski. He just needs work."

"He needs more than work," the man says. "He needs a miracle."

"I could be John Sobieski again!" John screams. He can see his life going down the drain right before his eyes. "Give me like, what?" He looks at the surgeon, who raises his eyebrows. "Say, half an hour in the Men's room? I could be John again!"

The surgeon loosens his scalpel in his shoulder holster, ready for action.

The casting guy thinks. "No," he says. "It's a ten second spot. Who needs it?"

John slumps, defeated.

"It's show business," the surgeon says. "Hey. There's lots of spots. Stick with it, John. Look at it this way. You'd have had to buy a whole new wardrobe."

John just looks at him. "No I wouldn't," he says. "My wife never throws anything away."

He turns to the casting assistant, begging now. "I *am* John Sobieski. Couldn't I just do, like, the voice over?"

Paul of the Theatre

After he dropped out of law school and then med school and then out of school altogether, Paul went into theatre. He took a weekend course in an old barn out in the country run by a couple of reconstructed hippies named Sunshine and Moonshine who were twins, brother and sister. You couldn't tell them apart except one of them had a beard. Nobody knew which one. After the course, he was as ready and qualified to go out and make theatre as anybody else around and he proceeded to do so.

It was a theatrical system that worked OK, except with teen-age kids. This was a bummer because, since he was just starting out, high schools tended to be one of his major markets. They paid well and nobody knew anything anyway so he was home free.

Unfortunately, the kids tended to be sceptical and uncooperative. They were reluctant to expose their deepest fears and dreams to a group, even to a group of their friends, in fact, particularly to a group of their friends.

They had the reasonable feeling that anything revealed would be used as a weapon against them at some later date. Probably just as they were about to jump into bed with the partner of their dreams, or at other moments of real weakness or need. They knew each other really very well.

Paul wouldn't admit it. "They're a bit blocked," he'd say, "but they'll come out of it. And once they do we'll see some really great work here."

Yeah, and hair would grow on a bowling ball some time soon, too.

Part 6

The Twyla Sisters

The Twyla sisters. Gloria and Natalie Twyla. When I knew them, anyway, they were what people used to call Siamese twins. But not identical twins. In fact, they were polar opposites. Except in sex, of course, and their taste in men.

They both liked the same kind of guy — nasty, brutish and short.

Gloria Twyla was about six six and weighed in at at least two-twenty. She didn't, but she looked as though she ought to, shave at least twice a day. Her sister, Natalie, was three foot eight and about sixty-two pounds soaking wet. Gloria wore her at her waist like a watch charm. Which is where they were joined — at the waist.

Since they were so different, they lived in separate apartments, adjoining and in the same building, but separate. They had an agreement to live in each apartment on alternate days. Which worked out OK except for the fact that they hated each other's taste in furniture, wallpaper and dishes so much that as soon as Gloria entered Natalie's apartment she went into a catatonic trance, and vice versa.

Now, it was OK for Gloria when this happened because she was so big in comparison with Natalie that she just moved around like she was alone. Had a whale of a time. However, it was hell for Natalie because, being attached to her sister and all was, for her, like trying to hold an ocean liner close to the dock all by herself with the tide going out. So, when Gloria was in Natalie's apartment Natalie spent most of her time in an oversized chair watching television and had to be fed and watered by friends.

It all got kind of complicated when, naturally, they both fell in love with the same guy. A Mr. Nasty, Brutish and Short if there ever was one. And he fell in love, so to speak, with both of them.

It was a pretty good deal for him. Because of their peculiar psychological makeup, neither one knew that he was cheating on her with the other because he visited each one in her own apartment. They might have suspected but they didn't know for sure.

When they went out in public, of course, both were wide awake. Mr. Nasty, Brutish and Short was in his glory. He used to like walking into the restaurants where he took them and being the centre of attention.

In fact, it wasn't a bad situation all around. Until they both got pregnant. It almost caused them to split up. Everybody accused everybody of seeing somebody else but, when they all had time to think about the matter, it became obvious. They were stuck with each other.

What he did was, he married Gloria, which put Natalie into a sulk until she realized that after two years she could claim, at least on alternate days of the week, common-law status, should such a thing be necessary.

Mr. Nasty, Brutish and Short was confused but didn't mind. It just meant that he couldn't take them out anywhere together because they'd fight all the time. But it was a situation he could live with.

And it was very clear, they weren't going to change.

Mr. Perfect

Ted Knipl was born perfect and it wasn't his fault. It wasn't anybody's fault. It just happened. It had to happen to somebody one day, right?

He was tall and muscular but not too muscular. Just right. He had a face like a statue of a Greek god, a wonderful smile, wavy hair, perfect teeth. Everything just the way it should be. Nothing to improve on, there.

He was intelligent, too. And good. Not just good-natured. Hell, any number of dogs are good-natured. He was deep down in the spirit good. A perfect goodness. The kind of young man your father used to be before your mother got to know him a little bit better.

He could fix a car, bake a lemon meringue pie, tart and lovely with the meringue just so. He could kick a football, wrestle, drink any three men under the table if he wanted to, (Not that he ever did that. That wasn't good and he was perfectly good.) recite his own poetry by the yard (sentimental stuff but, hey, not everybody likes Shakespeare, either) and more than carry a tune, accompanying himself on the banjo or the guitar. In short, he was a young man who just couldn't miss. A young man headed for greatness.

The only trouble was that (and it has to be admitted that this mattered around town even if it shouldn't), he had two heads. He was born with two perfect heads on one perfect body. His parents called the right hand head Ted and the left hand one Fred.

Ted was the athlete. If you needed anyone to run, jump, box, hit a baseball or swim then Ted was your head. Fred was the scholar and the artist.

His father doted on Ted but his mother favoured Fred. The girls in town didn't know what to think. He was so perfect but it seemed to them that maybe he was just too much of a good thing. They just didn't know. The jury was out on this.

Mary Jean Orkney, a beautiful, spiritual girl, consulted with her minister more than once just to find out if a two-headed man could be a true Christian.

Her minister didn't have the answer. He was afraid of how he would look if he wrote a letter about it to his superior. So the jury was still out on that, too.

In school, during exams, the teachers were all at a loss to know if Ted and Fred talking over the questions with each other was cheating. The principal was no help. He took one look at the lad, smiled slightly and walked softly away. No decision there, either.

But it all worked out for the good. Eventually, Ted (and Fred), married a woman who was always of two minds about everything. So they all fitted together perfectly and lived happily ever after. Why not? Some stories do end this way.

Biographical Notes

Charles Mountford is a poet and a researcher and lover of historical buildings who lives in Stratford, Ontario. His poems have been published in several magazines, including *Quarry, Prism International, The New Quarterly* and *Lamia Ink*, New York. He has won First Prize, in the short poem category, in The Alberta Poetry Contest. Also, he has written the libretto for an opera on the life of the renowned singer, John Boyden.

Colophon

This book is set in 10 pt Baskerville Old Face by Stephenson Blake. It is printed by desktop methods in short runs. The book will be reprinted at intervals to keep the title in print indefinitely.

This ink is water soluble: Protect your book from water stains!

This style of book production — intense computer use, office style printers, hand binding, low finished inventory and produce to demand — is adapted to the poetry book market in Canada, where demand is small but steady and prolonged. The challenge is not to make a lot of money, but to keep the book available to lovers of poetry for as long as possible. So to poetry lovers everywhere, this book is for you!

Printed and bound in Canada by Gavin Stairs, Gavin Stairs Fine Editions, for Pendas Productions.

Gavin Stairs Fine Editions
525 Canterbury Road
London, Ontario, Canada N6G 2N5
stairs@stairs.on.ca

Hand-made in Canada